THE COMPLETE GUIDE TO AIR CURTAINS

19 NAKED TRUTHS TO SAVE MONEY, SAVE ELECTRICITY AND GET SUPER PRODUCTIVITY ENVIRONMENT

THE COMPLETE GUIDE TO AIR CURTAINS

19 NAKED TRUTHS TO SAVE MONEY, SAVE ELECTRICITY AND GET SUPER PRODUCTIVITY ENVIRONMENT

MITUL JAIN

Published Internationally by
Pendown Press
Powered by Gullybaba.com

PENDOWN PRESS

Powered by **Gullybaba Publishing House Pvt. Ltd.,**

An ISO 9001 & ISO 14001 certified Co.,

Regd. Office: 2525/193, 1st Floor, Onkar Nagar-A, Tri Nagar, Delhi-110035, (From Kanhaiya Nagar Metro Station Towards Old Bus Stand)

Branch Office: 1A/2A, 20, Hari Sadan, Ansari Road, Daryaganj, New Delhi-110002

Ph.: 09350849407, 011-27387998

E-mail: info@pendownpress.com

Website: PendownPress.com

New Edition: 2020

Price:

ISBN: 978-93-89601-21-3

Layout Design: Pendown Press Publishing

CONTENTS

DEDICATION

I dedicate this book to the entire Mitzvah family, who have not only worked day in and day out, but also have assisted in so many ways to put the practical experience in this form of a book.

My family, for their endless support whenever I needed the most.

Manuj Bajaj, for motivating me to put all my knowledge and experiences on paper and write the book.

PREFACE

My journey to manufacturing of air curtains started in the year 2001 when people hardly used air curtains and were still learning about them. In the last few years, the market has grown, customers' needs have increased. The ever-changing scenario with respect to the market dynamics gives a new challenge to the industry every day. Spending 19 years in the industry, serving more than 13,000 customers and installing more than 1,50,000 air curtains has made me realise that people of different nations lack the knowledge about air curtains and its utilities.

Customers still do not know "what" exactly are air curtains, "why" to use them, "how" to select them and finally "where" to make the best use of them.

This encouraged me to write a book, to help people understand the benefits of this product.

Through this book, I want to raise awareness and shed light on the fact that how one can select the right model of an air curtain to save

- Money,
- Increase hygiene levels, and
- Improve his/her standard of living.

ACKNOWLEDGEMENTS

This entrepreneurial journey into different facets of business, right from manufacturing, designing, marketing to sales, has given me a lot of insight into business.

The launch of an innovative product two decades ago had given me insights into the various aspects of buying cycle, from a consumer point of view, right from Awareness, intention, desire to use the product.

In the last two decades, we have served approximately 13,000+ customers and more than 1,50,000 installations of air curtains have given me an insight into the various challenges faced by the customers and how to tackle them.

I would like to express my sincere gratitude to everyone who was a part of my journey; who supported and guided me, and helped me to come out with this book. My sincere thanks goes to:

Mitzvah Team, for their support and taking up challenges and find the most feasible solution.

Rahul Jain, my business coach, who has guided into streamlining the business processes and take it into a different orbit.

Manuj Bajaj, digital marketing coach, who pushed me to write this book.

Dinesh Goyal, my guru and guide during my initial training, was a pillar of strength.

Sushil Choudhary, my technical teacher who has been a father figure to me and always inspired to work harder.

ABOUT THE AUTHOR

Mitul is an Entrepreneur, Solution Strategist, Speaker. He is a first generation businessman who started the business from a mere seed capital of $100 and turned it into a successful manufacturing company with business across the globe.

He has been exceptionally successful at designing and executing various business operations by doing Business Process Reengineering and manoeuvring "Air" to increase Comfort, and reduction in maintenance and Power costs, and hence having a positive impact on the overall profitability of businesses.

He has an incredible wealth and depth of knowledge that is mostly derived from the first-hand experience while working in different industries.

- 19+years of experience in working with various segments.
- Degree in Mechanical Engineering, and a Masters in Business Administration.
- Worked Extensively on Energy Conservation on Hot Oven Application, and have given clients an Annual Saving of more than million Indian rupees.
- Worked with various organisations in varied applications like Bharat Electronics Limited, JCB, Taikisha, Honda,

Hindustan Aeronautics Limited, Metro, Airports and many more and helped them save energy and enhance comfort and hygiene.

- Worked on various out of the Box Business ideas, for both national and international market.
- Works extensively on Product Development and Innovation and has even developed "Air Curtains" for Buses in India, notable customers are Volvo and Tata Marcopolo.

Mitul's experience can be summarised as a person who has developed the organisational expertise to provide highly engineered services at optimum cost due to his microeconomic capabilities complemented with vast market knowledge, to give the ultimate benefit to the Customer.

ABOUT THE BOOK

This book raises awareness and throws light on the fact how one can select the right model of an air curtain to save money, increase hygiene level and improve his or her standard of living.

The book will guide its readers on a number of tips and solutions by using 'Air Curtain'. Everything related with air curtain is discussed at length and that too in lucid language and proper illustrations at suitable places.

Miscellaneous questions that may come in the minds of the readers are talked about in a separate chapter named as FAQs and answers relating to Air Curtains. No effort has been spared to make this book informative, illustrative, comprehensive, to-the-point and reader-friendly. However, some situations might have escaped attentions. We are quite receptive towards your valuable suggestions for the betterment of this mini book. We will incorporate your suggestions that merit inclusion with a sense of gratitude towards you.

1

WHAT IS AN AIR CURTAIN?

Before, actually getting into the specifics of how, what and where, it is quite crucial to understand what exactly are air curtains.

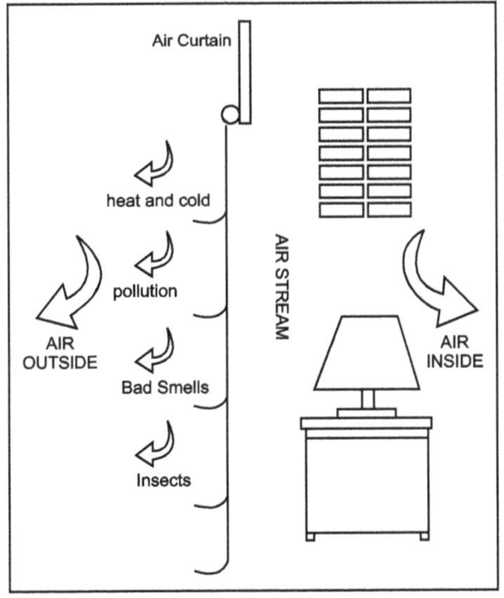

Fig. 1

Have you ever experienced air striking your head when you enter an airport or a mall? Ever wondered what that is? Well, it is surely something more than an ordinary door or any air vestibule. In fact, it is an invisible barrier of air that prevents the inside air to mix with the outside air, thus preventing the loss of conditioned air and obstruct the entry of mosquitoes, flies and dust, without any physical division.

Air curtains or air doors are devices that help create an unseen blockade between the air outside your premise and inside your workplace without the necessity of keeping a door which is a lot of hassle. Thus, air curtain is one of those devices

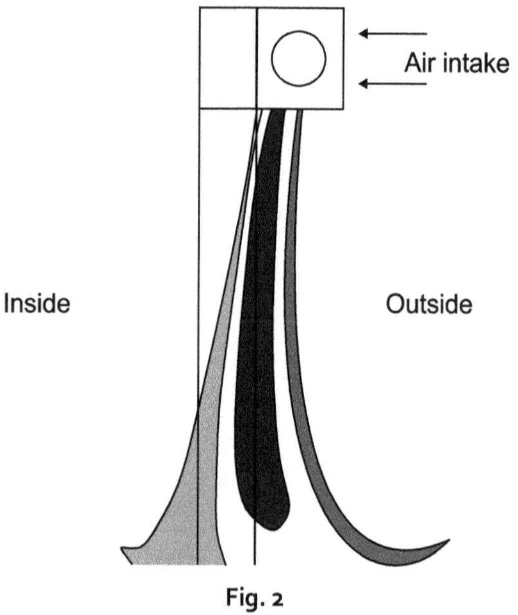

Fig. 2

that provides a lot of utility. This energy-saving innovation is used in commercial and residential buildings to prevent insects, dust and a wide range of other things from entering certain space. Furthermore, it ensures that the air in the building remains conditioned thereby, increasing the efficiency of the "air conditioners", by not allowing the air to escape. Other than that, it allows the owners to utilise the space near the doors that would otherwise be blocked by bulky vestibules etc. Air curtains generate a uniform stream of directed air, across an opening (as shown in Fig. 2) and creates a barrier that inhibits the transfer of heat and particulate matter from one zone to the other. An appropriately designed system will create this barrier across the entire height and width of the opening.

Broadly, air curtains are of two types:

1. Recirculating and
2. Non-circulating air curtains.

   The non-recirculating air curtain is more popular as it is more economical than the recirculating one.

   Recirculating air curtains are a complex assembly of fan, floor grills, baffle filters, hepa filters, duct and plenum to create a uniform flow. Thus, making installation difficult, time consuming and costly.

2

WHY DO WE NEED AN AIR CURTAIN?

In places such as airports, retail stores and manufacturing units with a continuous movement of either people, material or vehicles, a door wouldn't be a viable option as it would be necessary to leave the door open leading to the air, pests, dust and smell entering the conditioned environment. Air curtains provide an assurance of a well-sealed yet conditioned environment and offers a great level of comfort to the employees resulting in a happier workforce.

Moreover, in segments such as cold rooms, restaurants, hospitals, food and dairy industries, it is vital to protect the air inside from being contaminated by the air outside. Even during the stormy season, air curtains ensure to keep debris and other outside substances away thus maintaining hygiene and clean environment.

Controlling air transfer saves energy, enhances smooth and faster traffic flow, enhances the usability of spaces near doors and guarantees comfort. Air curtains deliver performance at its best for all and therefore, we need air curtains to maintain two separate outdoor and indoor environments by means of a thermal barrier without any physical structure existing between them.

In the further sections of the book, there will be a detailed analysis of the benefits.

3

HOW AN AIR CURTAIN WORKS AS A THERMAL BARRIER?

The Door or Shutter opens, if there is a thermal air temperature difference on both sides. The exchange of air starts, as seen in CFD Analysis diagram in Fig 3. Since the colder air is denser, it settles down and hot air rises up, since it is lighter. Now the cold

10 *Seconds after freezer door opens with Air Curtain* OFF

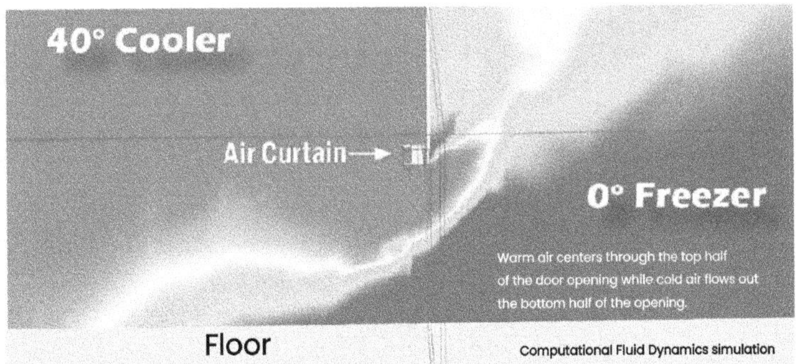

Fig. 3

air tries to move out from the bottom of the door and hot air moves towards the colder side from the top of the door.

This continuous exchange of air leads to heavy energy loss. Thus when the Air Curtain starts, as shown in CFD analysis diagram in Fig 4. It blows the air from top to bottom and creates an air wall along the width of the door, thus separating two different thermal conditions and acts like a barrier.

This leads to saving of conditioned air and inhibits the entry of dust, mosquitoes and flies.

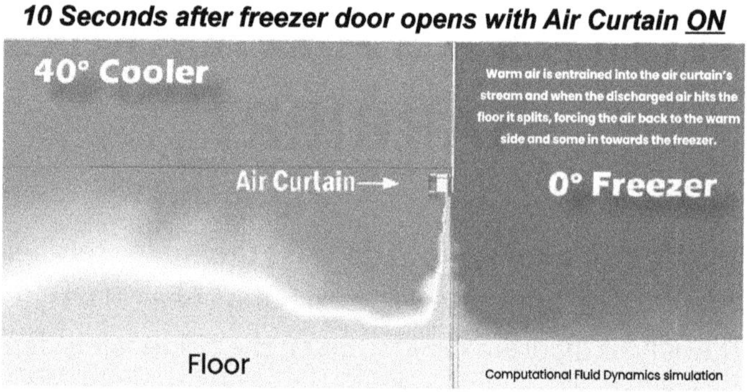

10 Seconds after freezer door opens with Air Curtain ON

40° Cooler

Warm air is entrained into the air curtain's stream and when the discharged air hits the floor it splits, forcing the air back to the warm side and some in towards the freezer.

Air Curtain→

0° Freezer

Floor

Computational Fluid Dynamics simulation

Fig. 4

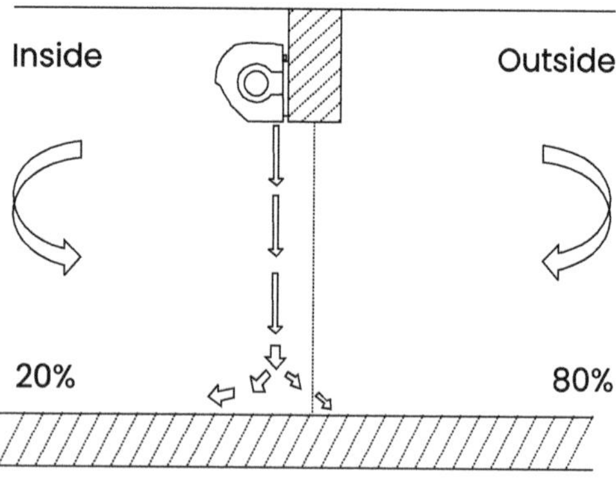

Fig.5

4

WHAT IS THE MECHANISM BEHIND AN AIR CURTAIN?

Air enters the Air Curtain (Air Door) through the fan housing before being accelerated by the fan. This fast moving air gets into the plenum which ensures that the air is evenly distributed along the entire length of the discharge nozzle.

The airfoil design of blower with vortex shaped housing in combination with the nozzle ensures the uniformity of the air stream and a minimum turbulence. The air which is discharged via the nozzle, goes to the floor as a jet stream and about 80% of the air volume gets to the side where the Air Curtain (Air Door) is installed or the suction side while 20% flows towards the opposite direction.

Or, in simpler words, we can say that the air curtains divide the internal and external environment.

It follows a complicated mechanism where the air enters the machine through an inlet grille attached inside the air curtain and then compressed by a few internal centrifugal fans (as visible in Fig. 6) and forced out through an air outlet, which is directed towards the open doorway.

Fig.6

Heated air curtains have a coil (electric, hot/chilled water, steam, indirect or direct gas, direct expansion, etc.) to heat or cool the jet. Heating is used to save people from feeling a cold jet of air while crossing the doorway and also, to heat the volume of air coming in at the entrance.

These types of air curtains are generally used in cold climates and are placed inside.

5

MOST COMMON PROBLEMS EXPERIENCED BY PEOPLE WHO ARE NOT USING AIR CURTAINS

In cold rooms, warehouses, industrial, commercial buildings and other such places, continuous movement is inevitable which means repeatedly opening and closing of doors and sending an open invitation to a variety of issues and problems.

People who do not invest in air curtains face common problems that might affect their daily operations;

a. Ingress of flies and mosquitoes
b. Heavy Electricity Bills
c. Air Conditioners not performing as desired
d. High Dust in the showroom
e. Smell or smoke problem

f. Continuous breakdown of Machines due to Dust & heating
g. Heavy loss of fuel in case of conveyor hot ovens
h. Worried about the opening and closing of the Door
i. Concerned about product Quality and hygiene
j. Irritated customers because of flies and mosquitoes.

This book will guide you on various tips and solutions to the above problems, by using 'Air Curtain'.

If you are also confused whether an air curtain will help you or not, then we have a very simple checklist in the next chapter that will help you identify the need for air curtain.

6

WHO NEEDS AIR CURTAINS?

Look at the checklist below and see if you face similar problems:

Checklist:

1. Does Dust affect you/your business?
2. Do you have Air Conditioned premises?
3. Do mosquitoes/Flies affect your comfort/product quality?
4. Does closing the door affect your inflow of customers?
5. Do you have conveyorised hot oven?
6. Do you want to reduce energy bills?
7. Do you have a Cold Room/Freezer/Chiller?

If the answer to any of the above is YES, then it is a must for you to have Air Curtains.

Efficacious in isolating the weather conditions, air curtains are a must for a variety of commercial as well as residential segments now.

It protects the air inside, wards off insects and dust, eliminating the need to buy products solely for the aforementioned purposes. Moreover, being a low- maintenance product, it provides a long-term cost-benefit effect and also maintains certain hygiene standards.

So in simple language, if you are a Business owner, Managing Director, Project manager or a Consultant of a Hotel, Restaurant, Pharma unit, Cold Room, food factory, warehousing unit or any other place and if comfort and hygiene are of prime importance to you and your business, you need an air curtain.

You can increase your business profitability and enhance your customer experience, by getting rid of mosquitoes, flies, dust and can save conditioned air from losing.

Generally, people invest a lot of energy and effort in planning and executing the design and construction of the project, but forget to consider the last feather in the cap, which becomes a leakage point in the building.

So if you are amongst them, don't make the same mistake. Become wiser and consider Air Curtains NOW !!

7

APPLICATIONS

Air Curtain can find its place in variety of Applications based on the major problems it solves for these segments. Here is a list of few places and major problems it solves for them.

Segments	Temp. Control	Dust Control	Flies Control
Bakery		✓	✓
Banks	✓	✓	
Banquet Hall	✓	✓	✓
Beverages	✓	✓	✓
Builders	✓	✓	✓
Call Centre	✓	✓	
Central Kitchen		✓	✓
Cold Storage	✓		
Cold Storage - Mobile Vans	✓		
Defence	✓	✓	
Entertainment Parks	✓	✓	✓
Frozen Food	✓	✓	✓

Government Building	✓	✓	
Hospital	✓	✓	✓
Hotel 2/3/4/5 Star	✓	✓	✓
Ice Cream Parlours	✓	✓	✓
Institutes / Colleges / School	✓	✓	
Liquor			
Manufacturers / Distributors		✓	✓
Malls	✓	✓	✓
Manufacturing - Automobiles	✓	✓	
Manufacturing - Beverages	✓	✓	✓
Manufacturing - Biscuit		✓	✓
Manufacturing - Bread		✓	✓
Manufacturing - Chemical	✓	✓	
Manufacturing - Consumer Durable			
Manufacturing - Cosmetics	✓	✓	
Manufacturing - Dairy	✓	✓	
Manufacturing - Electronics	✓		✓
Manufacturing - Engineering	✓	✓	
Manufacturing - Food		✓	
Manufacturing - Fragrances		✓	✓
Manufacturing - Paper	✓	✓	
Manufacturing - Plastic		✓	
Manufacturing - Rice		✓	
Manufacturing - Shoes		✓	✓
Manufacturing - Sugar		✓	
Manufacturing - textile		✓	✓
Manufacturing - Thermoforming		✓	
Medical - Diagnostic Centre		✓	
& Path Lab	✓	✓	✓

Medical - Hospital	✓	✓	✓
Mid Day Meal		✓	✓
Pharmaceutical Units	✓	✓	✓
Poultry Farms			✓
Processing - Meat	✓	✓	✓
Railways	✓	✓	
Religious Place	✓	✓	✓
Residence			
Restaurant	✓		✓
Retail Store	✓	✓	
Showroom - Automobiles	✓	✓	
Tent House	✓		✓

8

WHAT ARE THE VARIOUS TYPES OF AIR LOSSES IN A BUILDING?

There are three prime mechanisms through which conditioned air contained inside is lost via an opening in a building;

1. Natural Convection
2. Natural Ventilation
3. Mechanical Ventilation

Let's discuss what they are and how to combat the issues with the help of air curtains.

Natural Convection

Cold air is denser than warm air, which allows cold air to settle down. Across an unimpeded boundary between a heated and a cool area, conditioned cool air will escape from the bottom of the opening. This process will naturally allow Hot Air to enter the conditioned space, from the top of the opening, which is known as natural convection.

This process happens due to the thermal properties present *i.e.* the tendency of a hotter and hence, less dense air to rise and a colder air to sink under the influence of gravity resulting in transfer of heat into the surroundings.

Under these conditions, an air curtain can limit the exchange of air between the two zones by creating a barrier to impede air flow.

The turbulent flow of air curtain creates a secondary layer that makes Air Curtains work effectively and also affect the natural air flow pattern in the thermal convection.

Natural Ventilation

An airtight building is never possible. There is invariably some openings and crevice, such as doors, windows and cracks that prove to be the facilitator of cold air to pass as well as hot air to enter in the building in order to replace it through the mechanism as very well explained in the previous process.

The prevailing wind conditions and directions can exacerbate this natural ventilation mechanism, relative to the openings.

In this type of situation, the use of an air curtain can reduce the ill effects of air loss as a natural consequence of wind-driven natural ventilation, through the doorways. Air Curtains have got the ability to work wonderfully well on Doorways and can reduce the losses significantly on conditioned Air and prevent entrance of mosquitoes, flies and dust.

Mechanical Ventilation

The mechanical ventilation, also referred to as artificial ventilation, uses artificial fans, such as Ventilation System, Exhaust Fans, Gravity Ventilators and several more.

A region within a building, or the interior of a building, can be very well pressurised under the three separate conditions:

a. Pressurised positively, where the Air is moving out of the area in consideration
b. Pressurised negatively, where the Air is moving in the area in consideration
c. Non-pressurised (with no pressure differential between zones).

   All these variations in pressure difference across an opening between zones can be its natural consequence of a poorly balanced ventilation system, ineffective controls or in few cases of a well-thought design decision.

   Air curtain solutions have the ability to work in almost all of these scenarios (controlled conditions). The Flow of Air Curtains is hugely affected if there is properly ventilated building. Nonetheless, they are most effective if the pressure differential across the air stream is minimum.

9

ARE AIR CURTAINS EFFECTIVE?

No doubt they are!

Various studies and research conducted show that Air Curtains are effective in creating a barrier to keep the inside air well conditioned.

It has been determined that the cooling power loss (Q) kW from an open cold storage/conditioned doorway, because of infiltration of air, can be calculated using the following expression by Mann/Hofer.

$$Q = (0.48 + 0.004\Delta T)\, A\, (h_w - h_c\, \sqrt{Hp_c}\, \sqrt{1 - \frac{P_w}{P_c}}$$

Where,

ΔT = temperature differential across doorway (°C)

A = area of doorway (m^2)

h_w = enthalpy of air on warm side of doorway (kJ/kg)

h_c = enthalpy of air on cold side of doorway (kJ/kg)

ρ_c = density of air on cold side of doorway (kg/m³)

ρ_w = density of air on warm side of doorway (kg/m³)

H = height of doorway (m)

As an example a cold store with a 2.35m high x 1.8m wide doorway has a cold store temperature of minus 22°C with 70% relative humidity. The loading bay area adjacent to the cold store is typically at +7°C, 70% Rh. This equates to a cooling load of 69kW which has to be made up by the cold store refrigeration equipment.

Research has been carried out with FRPERC, University of Bristol, where tests were carried out with a cold store air curtain fitted over the doorway of a cold store. The infiltration of air into the cold store was measured using a CO_2 tracer gas method for different door opening times with and without the air curtain operating. From these tests the effectiveness of the air curtain in preventing infiltration of air was as high as 76.9%, where effectiveness E can be described by the following equation:

$$E = \frac{Q_b - Q_a}{Q_b}$$

Where,

E is the Energy Effectiveness,

Q_a is the Energy Exchange through an Open Doorway With an Air Curtain fitted plus the power consumed by the Air Curtain,

Q_b is the Energy Exchange through an Open Doorway WITHOUT an Air Curtain fitted,

The closer the Energy Effectiveness is to 1 (unity) the better the energy effectiveness

with, 1 = Ultimate Barrier (equivalent to a closed door, if $Q_a = 0$)

0 = Bad (equivalent to an open doorway with no air curtain, if $Q_a = 1$)

In this case example, the cooling load of 69kW would be reduced to 15.9kW (*i.e.* 69kW x 0.231) with a decrease in electricity costs and a reduction in health and safety hazards from ice formation and fog in the doorway.

Reference studies done by HEVAC members, BSRIA (UK) and by TNO (Netherlands).

The above example proves the enormous savings which can be achieved by installing the air curtains on the doorway. However, it is equally important to choose the right velocity at the right height

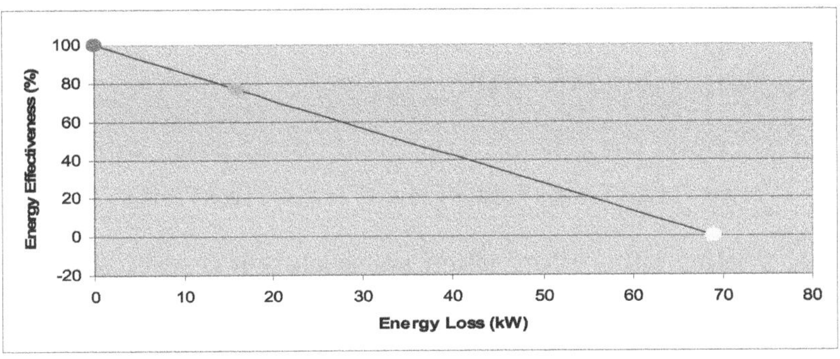

Fig. 7

to achieve the desired result. An Air curtain, if not chosen properly, will accelerate the loss of conditioned air. The same can be seen in figure 9, which is a descriptive model, between the strength of the air stream of the air curtain and the cooling in the chamber.

Further, the air curtain effectiveness can be seen with the help of following figure...

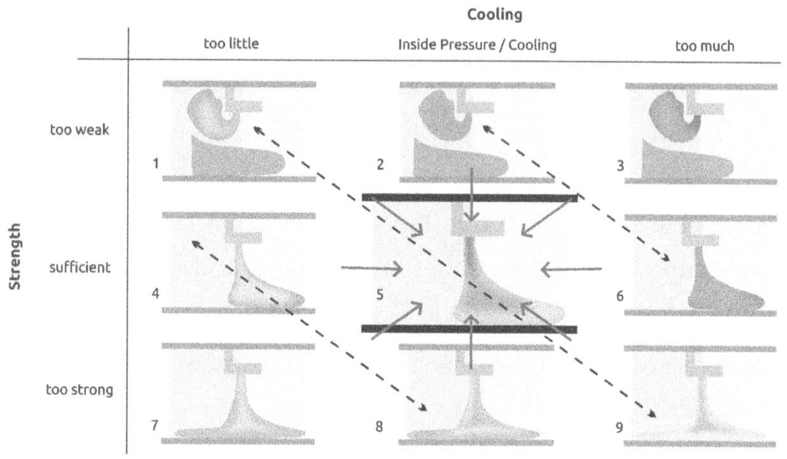

Air Curtain Strength and Cooling Control Protective

Fig. 8

Clockwise from top left:

Fig. 1 shows the effect on the conditioned space without an air curtain and illustrates convective heat losses,

Fig. 2 shows the effect when an air curtain is used with too high an airflow velocity,

Fig. 3 shows the effect when an air curtain is used with incorrect outlet angle,

Fig. 4 shows the effectiveness of a correctly installed and selected air curtain

21-22
20-21
19-20
18-19
17-18
16-17
15-16
14-15
13-14
12-13
11-12
10-11
9-10
8-9
7-8
6-7
5-6
4-5
3-4
2-3
1-2
0-1

20-21
19-20
18-19
17-18
16-17
15-16
14-15
13-14
12-13
11-12
10-11
9-10
8-9
7-8
6-7
5-6
4-5
3-4
2-3
1-2
0-1

20-21
19-20
18-19
17-18
16-17
15-16
14-15
13-14
12-13
11-12
10-11
9-10
8-9
7-8
6-7
5-6
4-5
3-4
2-3
1-2
0-1

20-21
19-20
18-19
17-18
16-17
15-16
14-15
13-14
12-13
11-12
10-11
9-10
8-9
7-8
6-7
5-6
4-5
3-4
2-3
1-2
0-1

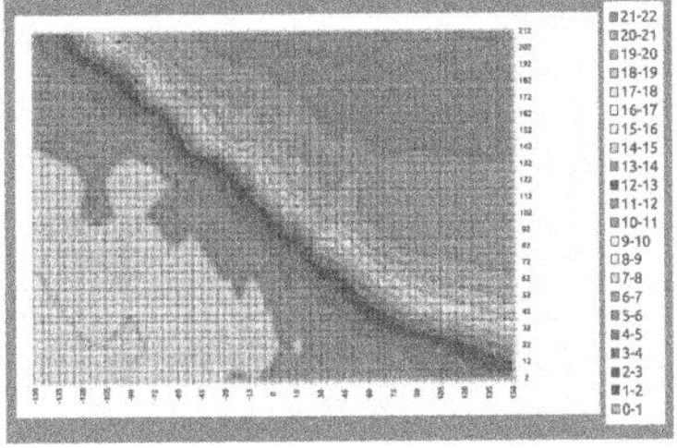

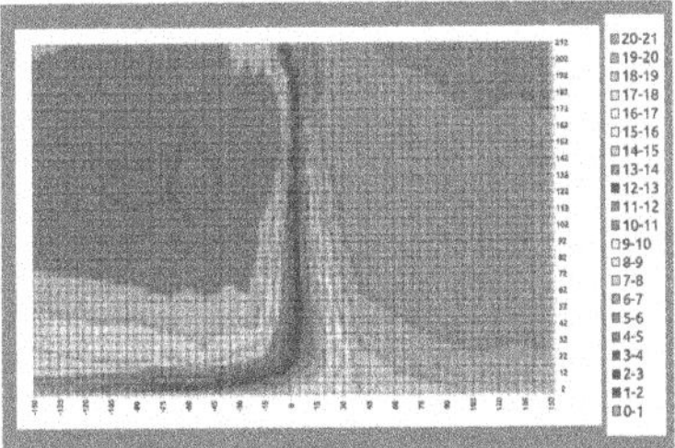

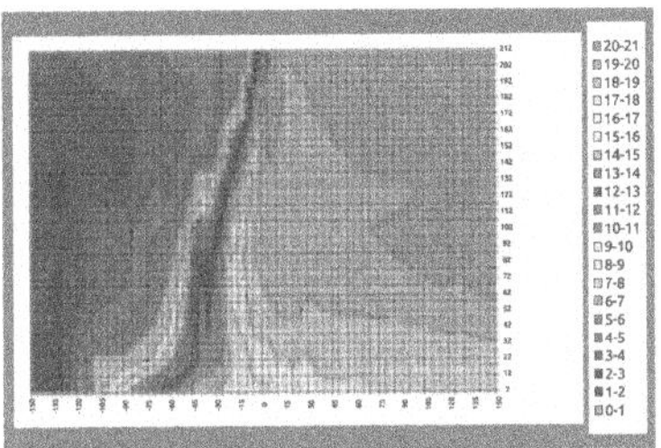

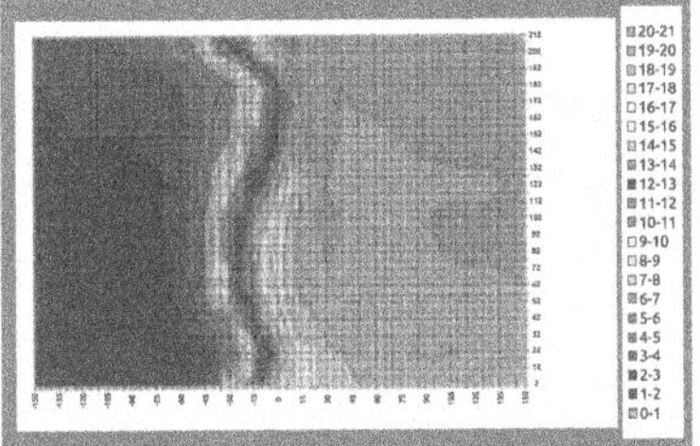

Fig. 9

10

ADVANTAGES OF AIR CURTAINS

An air curtain is a versatile product which is useful in a variety of domains. It is a multi-utility machine that can be used as a solution for a variety of problems that we face on a daily basis.

Air curtains offer many advantages because of which they are common in many industries and across various segments. Air curtains are available in a variety of sizes and can be installed in various ways to give the desired results. Installing an air curtain in your business is the best move that will mitigate your vast range of concerns.

There are numerous benefits of installing Air curtains in your work areas and these benefits can be categorized into Primary benefits and Secondary benefits.

5 Major Primary Benefits of Air Curtains Include:

1. **Environmental Separation:** Air curtain forms a barrier that prevents air to cross over to the other side. The outside

environment usually has all kinds of uncomfortable odors and pollutants. It is especially very difficult to prevent bad odors and fumes in areas that are closer to industrial plots, garbage area or treatment plants. By preventing any unwanted infiltration of dust, outdoor odors and pollutants, air curtains help maintain a pleasant environment in the facility.

2. **Temperature Control:** Temperature difference in two areas will naturally create an air transfer between these two areas. Warm air will escape from top of the doorway and will be replaced by cold denser air entering from the bottom side. A greater temperature difference will only result in higher air infiltrations and energy losses. Air curtains prevent this exchange by protecting the conditioned environments in different areas and help control the temperature.

3. **Saves Money:** We all know that inducing a change of temperature requires a lot of money. For example- if we are inducing hot air in the oven, we require burners and fuel to do it. Similarly for cooling the air, we need AHU (Air Handling Units), Chillers or Freezers. Whenever this conditioned air gets wasted or is lost, it results in increasing our overall cost. By providing an effective barrier for conditioned air, Air curtains offer an ideal solution to save your money.

4. **Insect and Pest Control:** Flying insects and bugs can be a nuisance for anyone. The presence of these insects within an area can lead to food contamination, unhealthy conditions and other associated problems. The powerful

Fig. 10

stream of air produced by an Air Curtain prevents these harmful pests and other flying insects from entering the premises and thereby maintains hygienic and sanitary conditions for everyone.

5. **Works in Extreme Conditions:** Air curtains create an invisible barrier that isolates different temperature zones without hindering the movement of people and products. Many industries use heating appliances or ovens while others use cold storage and other cooling systems. Air curtains work in both the conditions by effectively sealing the area and preventing the air exchange and energy loss.

    a. **Blast Freezer/Chillers/Cold Storage:** Air curtains are highly beneficial for cold storage as it can greatly reduce the energy loss by keeping the chilled air in and warm air out with the door open and in use. Air curtains are known to reduce losses by up to 90%.

a. **Hot Ovens:** Air curtains have proved advantageous for industries using hot ovens and industrial conveyors. They can be used to hold extreme heat and contain hot air inside on the industrial conveyor or oven. This has resulted in fuel savings of up to 40% of the total oven fuel consumption.

Along with the above mentioned primary benefits, there are also 9 other secondary benefits provided by air curtains as mentioned below:

1. **Protects Product Quality:** The protective barrier provided by an Air curtain keeps harmful chemicals away from your valuable products and machinery. This

Fig. 11

reduction in pollution reduces the wear and tear of parts and other useful machinery and maintains the quality of your product.

2. **Saves Manpower:** Air curtains provide a barrier against airborne dust, pollution, fumes and bad odors. Less dust and pollutants from outside reduce the need for continuous cleaning and maintaining the facility thereby reducing the manpower requirement for the facility. Some places where it can directly impact are retail stores, show rooms etc.
3. **Drop in Factory Accidents:** Closed glass door or doors with obstructions are a potential threat to staff and potential customers. Air curtains provide a risk-free alternative by shielding the premises without obstructing the vision.
4. **Open Door Policy:** An open door is always an invitation to customers and thus, advisable but an open door also invites unwanted particles like dust, insects, bad odors and other pollutants. With an air curtain, you can enjoy all the benefits of an open door without incurring any of its limitations and also save on the manpower costs needed to frequently operate a physical door.
5. **Saves Power:** With Air curtains, energy loss through doorways is drastically reduced. Reduced energy loss decreases the load on existing temperature control systems like air conditioners, heaters or ovens and helps save power.
6. **Lowers Maintenance Cost:** Reduced dust and pollutants ensures the quality of products and since there is a

reduction in leakage of conditioned air, the Duty cycle reduces for the machines. This reduction in Duty Cycle increases the lifespan of air conditioners, chillers, blast freezers and others temperature control machines.

7. **Odor Control:** The steady air stream from an air curtain forms a protective barrier and keeps bad odors out. This helps maintain a clean and hygienic environment that invites more customers and improves the overall image of your brand.

8. **Increase in Business Efficiency:** By avoiding leakage of conditioned air and keeping the mosquitoes and flies away, air curtains help increase the comfort level of both external customers and internal employees. Comfortable environment and satisfied employees result in increasing the overall business efficiency.

9. **Cash Cow:** Air Curtains can be termed as cash cows for a business as they give a steady return on profits that exceeds the money invested in acquiring it. In general air curtains have an ROI of less than 3 months.

11

TECHNOLOGICAL EDGE OF AIR CURTAINS

Classification of Air Curtains Based on Flow and Fans Type

Air curtains can be mainly classified into two types:

a. Recirculating and
b. Non-recirculating Air curtains

Recirculating Air Curtain gathers and returns the discharged air in the air curtains inlet. The process is continuously repeated with a plenum built into the floor that connects back to the inlet of the air curtain via duct. (as shown in Fig. 5)

Non-recirculating Air Curtain captures fresh air from the environment and discharges it from the unit. Since the same air is not recirculated back, these air curtains can be termed as non-recirculating air curtains.

AIR CURTAIN UNIT
AIR RETURN
SEAL
AIR
FLOW
AIRSTREAM
DISCHARGE
OUTSIDE
INSIDE
ENTRAINED AIR
ENTRAINED AIR
AIR STREAM
AIR
FLOW

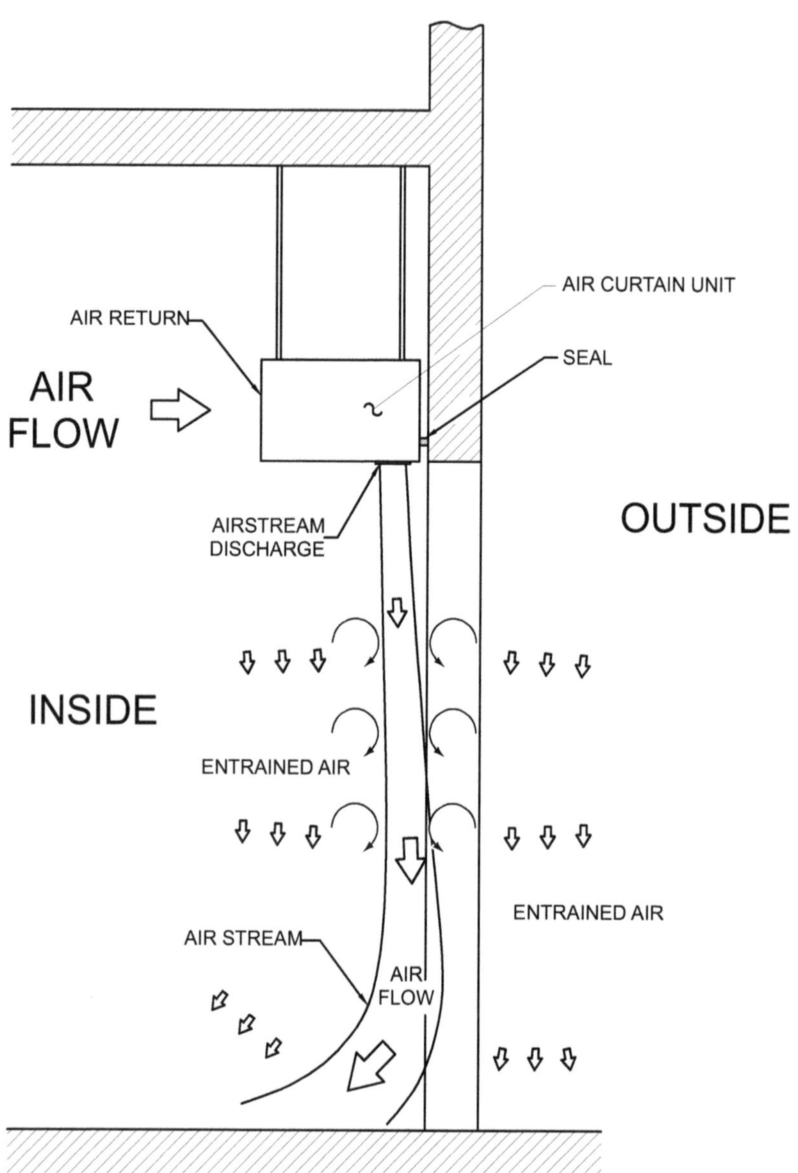

Fig. 13

OUTSIDE
AIR RETURN PIT
DISCHARGE
PLENUM
AIR STREAM
ENTRAINED AIR
AIR
FLOW
STRAIGHTENING
SECTION
AIRSTREAM
DISCHARGE
ENTRAINED AIR
INSIDE
FLOOR GRATING

DISCHARGE
PLENUM
AIR
FLOW
AIR RETURN PIT
DUCTWORK
AIR HANDLER
DRAIN

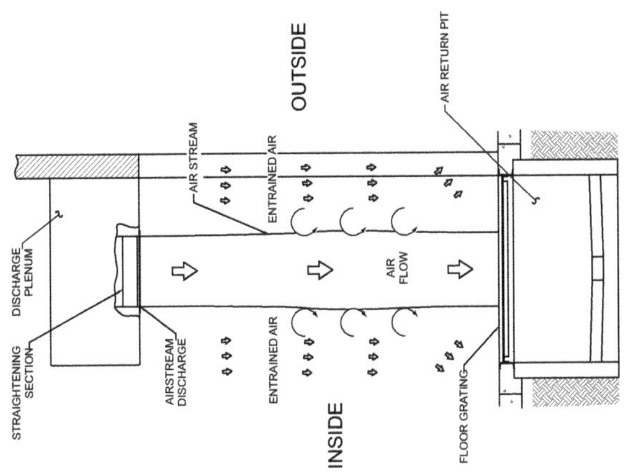

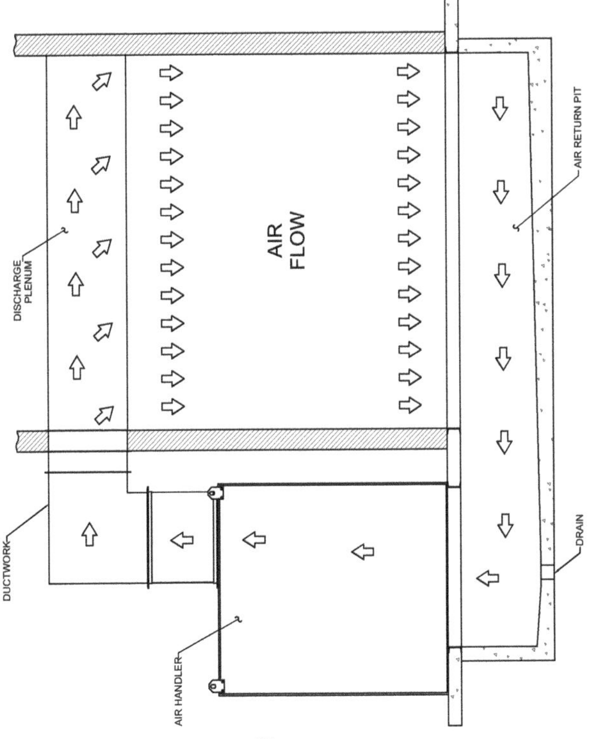

Fig. 14

Recirculating air curtains are more efficient than their counterparts but still, non-recirculating air curtains are more popular. Majority of installations today are non-recirculating due to their cost efficiency and ease of installation.

Directions of Flow:

There are 3 possible directions of blow-out air streams, both for recirculating and non-circulating curtains:

- **Horizontal Mounting from top to bottom:** Horizontal mounting is the most common Installation and most economical way to mount an air curtain. Here, the air curtain is installed horizontally across the top of the opening and the air is discharged from top to bottom of the door.
- **Vertical Mounting from left to right or right to left:** Here, the curtain is mounted perpendicular to the ground and the air is expelled from left to right and right to left. Vertical discharge mostly requires mounting curtains on both sides of the door which adds up the total cost of installation. Normally, this kind of installation is required in places in very wide or high door openings.
- **Horizontal discharge from bottom to top:** This installation is not very common and specially used in case of hot oven applications. The curtain units require special frames and are mounted at the floor level and the installation is carried out under specialized guidance.

Type of Fans

Air Curtains can be designed and manufactured with various types of Fans. Three most commonly used fan types are:

Centrifugal

Most of the air curtain units employ centrifugal fans that use a forward or backward-curved impeller. Centrifugal fans make use of blades to drag air into a circular motion. The pressure of an incoming airstream is increased by blades mounted on a circular hub and alters the direction of the outward flowing air, usually by 90°. Centrifugal fans move air radially and outwards through the vortex housing. Centrifugal fans provide a stronger and more stable air flow than axial fans and therefore, need a higher power input.

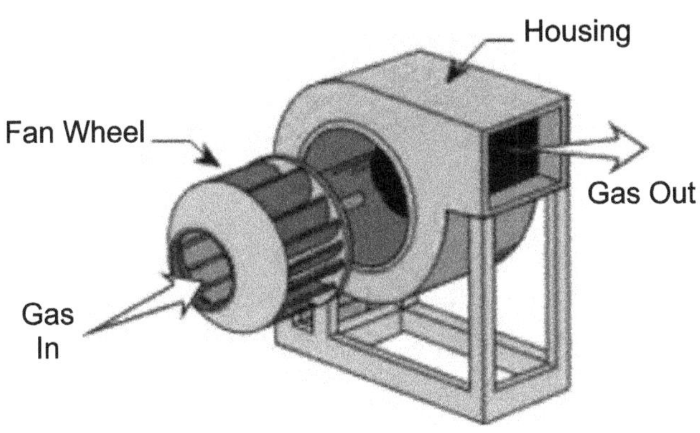

Fig. 15

Axial

As the name suggests, an Axial fan causes air to flow through it in an axial direction. The fan blades rotate around an axis and draw air in parallel to that axis. In other words, the air flows axially in and axially out which forces the air out in the same direction. The fan creates a pressure difference that forces flow through the fan.

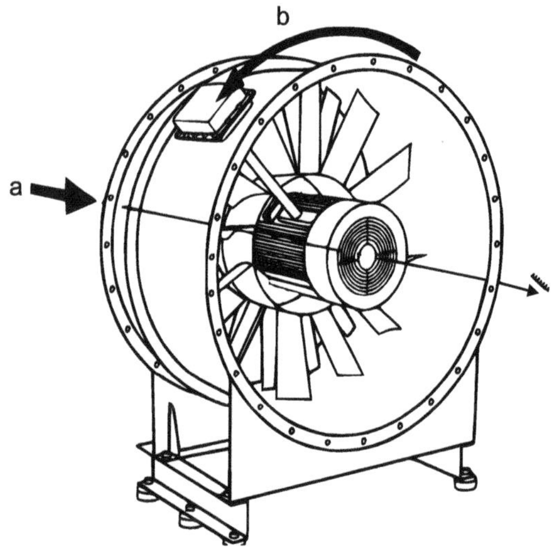

Fig. 16

Axial fans create a large volume of airflow, but the airflows they create are of low pressure. Therefore, these fans need a low power input for operation. There is a wide range of axial flow fans. It may vary from low or medium pressure fans to high-pressure fans. Because of the cool and low-pressure high-volume airflows they create, axial fans are best suited for many general purpose applications.

Cross Flow

Cross flow fans are derivative fans and comprises of housing with a rear wall and a vortex wall. Within that housing, there is an impeller surrounded by forward curved blades. When the air moves through a cross flow fan, it flows transversely and passes through its blades twice.

In Cross Flow fans, the air enters in a perpendicular direction to the motor shaft and is deflected by the fan blades and expelled. These fans have a long, rectangular shape and use either an alternating current (AC) or direct current (DC) motor. These fans are also referred to as tubular fans or tangential fans because of their long and narrow shape and air flow pattern. Unlike centrifugal fans, in cross flow fans the air flows through the fan itself rather than through an inlet. They provide high-pressure coefficient and are preferred for their low noise. The most common application for them is split air conditioner.

All the above types of fan have their own advantages and disadvantages and can be used for different kinds of applications.

12

PARAMETERS TO CONSIDER BEFORE CHOOSING AN AIR CURTAIN

There are two primary questions that need to be answered and understood:

1. Will Air Curtain work for me ?
2. What are the parameters required to choose the Right Model ?

   Basically, there is very limited information you require to decide on the requirement of the air curtain:

   The Basic information required to know, whether air curtain will be suitable for your facility or not, are as follows:

a. Width and Height of the Opening
b. Negative Pressure in the facility
c. Outside Wind Draft
d. Purpose of Installation
    i. Insect Control
    ii. Dust Control
    iii. Save Conditioned Air
    iv. Odour Control

    With these basic information, we can judge whether the air curtains will work for us or not.

3. Factors affecting the selection of air curtains can be classified into 2 categories:
    a. Primary Parameters.
    b. Secondary Parameters.

Primary Parameters	**Secondary Parameters**
Type	Voltage
Flow	MOC Blower
Mounting	MOC Chassis
Fan	Operation
Placement	

The Primary Parameters include a variety of options that affect the performance of an Air curtain like:

Type

a. Recirculating
b. Non-recirculating

Flow

As discussed above, there are three types of flow:

- Top to Bottom
- Sideways (L to R, R to L)
- Bottom to top

Mounting

Surface Mounted

Recessed

Fan

There are three types of fans to choose from:

- Centrifugal
- Crossflow
- Axial

Placement

Inside

Outside

The air curtain can be easily mounted on either side; whether inside or outside the conditioned area. Usually, it is recommended that the equipment should be installed towards the warmer side for optimum results. It implies, when installing a heated air curtain under cold conditions, it should be installed Inside. Places where the temperatures are too high and the major problem are dust, flies and saving the cold air, it should be installed outside to get the best results.

Even the secondary factors play an equally important role in the selection of an air curtain. They include:

Voltage

The voltage output plays a major role in the selection of air curtains as these machines are specially designed to operate with the mentioned amount of electric outputs. For Indian markets, air curtains are designed with respect to these three outputs:

- 220V/ 1 phase/50Hz
- 220V/ 1 phase/60Hz
- 440V/ 3 phase/50Hz

  Otherwise, for the Saudi Market, curtains that work with 220 V 1 P 60 Hz output are demanded. Air curtains can also be installed in buses and are specially built for 24 V/ DC. Thus, information on voltage is important for picking out the right air curtain for you.

MOC for blower

MOC or the "Material of Cover" for the blower is another specification on the basis of which air curtains are selected. The covers are made of different materials to suit different requirements, such as:

- Galvanised Iron
- Plastic
- Stainless Steel

- Aluminium

MOC for Chassis

Chassis basically refers to the main mounting and the fixing plate of an air curtain. For the chassis, the customer usually has two options of either picking one of the two materials;

- Stainless Steel 304 or
- CRC Powder Coated

  An air curtain consultant can help you in picking between various options.

Operation

- Switch Operated
- Remote

  Automatic coupled with the Door

  To find help in choosing the air curtains, you can go and visit www.mitzvah.in or choose one from the online store www.mitzvah.in/store

13

HOW TO TAKE SIZES FOR AN AIR CURTAIN?

Contrary to the common belief, taking measurement is actually a child's play. With only single equipment, *i.e.* a measuring tape, this job can be done easily. It is important to know just 3 basic pointers:

1. Width of the door
2. Height of the door
3. Space available above the door Checklist/Selection Guide

   You can even go to the link to watch the video- https://youtu.be/JcrGHe_NE04

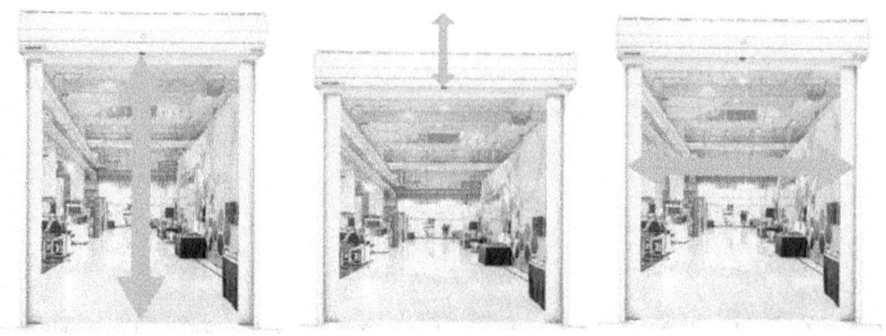

Fig. 17 Fig. 18 Fig. 19

14

FACTORS THAT WILL DRASTICALLY HAMPER THE AIR CURTAIN'S PERFORMANCE

Factors that hamper the Effectiveness of Air Curtains

Typically air curtains work well in many facilities such as production and industrial buildings, stores, transport terminals, car services, garages, markets, shopping complexes, drying houses etc. But proper installation of air curtains is necessary to ensure its proper working.

There are few other factors that can affect the efficient working of air curtains such as:

1. **Negative Pressure:** If the facility has exhaust fans or gravitational ventilators and no supply air or there is a difference between the exhaust and supply air (*i.e.* the

latter is less than the former) the negative pressure is created.

2. In these kinds of conditions the volume of air moving out from air curtains is also sucked in the facility along with the outside air and hence air curtains become ineffective.
3. **High Wind Velocity:** When the outside Wind Velocity is too high as in the case of storms, it will disrupt the flow pattern created by the air curtain on the doorway. So, whenever the outside wind velocity becomes greater than the velocity of the curtain, it will get disrupted.
4. **Horizontal Gap between Wall and Machine:** If the horizontal gap between the wall and the machine is too wide, the performance of air curtains will be drastically reduced. An air curtain should be installed close enough to the door so that there is no leakage from the sides of the door. The gap should be less than 50mm, for maximum effectiveness.
5. **Vertical Gap between the Nozzle and the top of the Door:** If the vertical gap between the nozzle and top of the opening will be wide, the effectiveness of the air curtain will be affected. Ideally, the gap should be less than 100 mm.machine.
6. **Sizing the Air Curtain:** The Air Curtain should always be equal to the Width of the Door, for it to perform optimally. If the air curtain is oversized, it will require more energy than usual and if the air curtain is undersized, it will prove insufficient to fully protect the opening it has

been installed above. This will lead to an unnecessary increase in costs because of energy wastage.

7. **Placement of Air Curtain:** When our primary objective is to discourage entry of mosquitoes and flies, the air curtain should be installed outside. When installed outside, it becomes 4 times more effective to stop flies, than the one which is installed inside.

15

HOW TO SAVE RS. 420 EVERY HOUR AND ENHANCE PRODUCTIVITY?

Air is nature's greatest gift to mankind and the quality of air we breathe in affects not only our productivity but the quality of our life as well. Air curtains are one of the best and most cost-effective ways to maintain the quality of air within the premises and retain a hygienic environment.

Do you know air curtains can help us save millions of hard-earned money?

A simple mathematical calculation can prove this. Let's see how:

Energy Calculation

$E = m\,C\,\Delta T$

m : Mass of Air

C : Specific heat of Air at given Temperature

ΔT : Temperature Difference

m = Density x Volume

Density of Air at 40˚C = 1.127 Kg/cu. Meter .... A

C = Specific Heat = 1.005 KJ / (Kg ˚C)

ΔT = Temperature difference = 15˚C

(assuming outside temperature is 40˚C and inside is 25˚C)

Volume = Area x Velocity of Air from Door x Time of Opening

Say :

Door Size = 8ft x 4ft

Velocity = 1 m/s = 200 fpm

Time of Opening = 1 min

Volume = 32 x 200 x 1 = 6400 cu. ft. = 181.22 cu.

Meter .... A

m = Density x Volume

(from Above A B) = 1.127 Kg/cu. meter 181.22 cu.

Meter = 204 Kgs

E = m C ΔT

= 204 kgs x 1.005 KJ / (Kg ˚C) x 15˚C = 3075.3 KJ = 0.85425 KWh

Thus :

In India if Per KWH cost of Power is Rs. 8.10

Cost of Opening the Door of Size 8ft x 4ft for 1 min is = Rs. 6.92

Cost of Running an Air Curtain of 4 ft = 400W (Input Power) for 1 minute = 6 paise

Rate per Kwh x Time x Power Input

8.10 x 1/60 x 0.4 = 5.4 paisa

Net Saving = Rs. 6.92 - 0.06 = Rs. 6.86 ~ Rs. 7

Saving per Hour = Rs. 7 x 60 min = Rs. 420 per Hour

Thus, you can see how Air Curtains help us save Rs. 420/hour. Also, they create a comfortable and amiable environment by keeping mosquitoes, flies and other pollutants away.

An air curtain helps maximize the savings by reducing energy loss and improving the effectiveness of our cooling/ heating systems. They provide a risk-free alternative by shielding the premises without an actual physical door and are one of the best investments for a business.

16

THINGS THAT EVERY CONSULTANT SHOULD KNOW BEFORE DRAFTING THE SPECIFICATION

9 things every consultant should know about Air Curtains:

1. **Speed is not the only way to measure Air Curtains:** The output of the air curtain device is measured in terms of velocity of air. The input power is varied and efforts are made to optimise the performance of the air curtain device.

2. **Static Pressure plays a significant role in selection of the Air Curtain:** Your selection depends upon the frictional force that occurs when you try to push an object alongside a surface. Static Pressure is a pressure of fluid on a body when the latter is at rest relative to it.

3. **Air Curtain does not work in all the Wind Conditions:** Like if the air pressure outside is more than that of the pressure inside, then the air curtain won't work properly.
4. **In Hot Conditions, Air Curtain should be generally Installed Outside:** Air curtains are designed for indoor installations (environment: normal, basic) above or next to the door. Typical installation sites are production and industrial buildings, stores, transport terminals, car services, garages, markets, drying houses etc.
5. **Air Curtains will not work in a negative pressurized building:** Air doors work best when the pressure differential between the inside and outside of the building is as close to neutral as possible. Negative pressure, extreme temperature differences, elevators in close proximity, or extreme humidity can reduce the effectiveness of air doors.
6. Impeller **Diameter** and **RPM** play a major role in deciding the flow pattern.
7. **Air Curtains can be used to prevent Cold Air from escaping as in Blast Chillers to Hot Air in Ovens:** Air doors are often used where doors are required to stay open for operational purposes, such as loading docks and vehicle entrances. They help keep outside air, thus reducing infiltration through the opening. Cold draft can be avoided by mixing in warm air heated by the air door. Heated air doors are commonly used when supplemented heat is needed for a space and to reduce the wind chill factor, inside the opening in colder climate.

8. **Centrifugal Vs Cross Flow:** Centrifugal Technology works best in non heated Air Curtains Cross flow. Technology is generally used in Heated Air Curtain.
9. **Value of Opening a Door:** Whenever a Door Opens for a Minute you lose Rs. 7 of Conditioned Air. Generally Air Curtains can be coupled with Limit Switch so that whenever a Door Opens Air Curtain Operates.

17

THINGS TO CONSIDER BEFORE SELECTING A VENDOR

Selecting a vendor is one of the most crucial tasks before selecting an air curtain. A reliable vendor will understand your needs and help you choose the air curtain that is best suited to your requirements. There are various important factors listed below that you must consider before selecting your vendor:

1. **Manufacturer:** You should know the original source *i.e.* from where your vendor procures the machines. The manufacturer must be a reputed one in the field and enjoy great goodwill in the market.
2. **Experience:** To a great extent, the experience of the vendor decides his reliability. Better experience implies better understanding and knowledge of market conditions and customer's requirement. Therefore, it

becomes imperative to analyse the experience of the vendor.

3. **Number of Installations:** Choose the vendor who has already served for a number of years. Get to know the number of installations done by them within the country and around the world (if any). A large number of installations would imply better knowledge and better understanding in the field.
4. **Technically Equipped:** Their production unit should be technically advanced in terms of working and delivery. It will provide a better breakthrough in the competitive market. The vendor should be able to guide you on various kinds of flow patterns and workability and should be able to customise a solution whenever required.
5. **Warranty and Part Availability:** Many vendors commit a warranty that is beyond their scope. As an international standard, a manufacturer should be able to provide support for all the parts and make them available for a minimum tenure of 10 years. Generally, traders overcommit and shed their responsibility when parts are needed.

18

RIGHT VELOCITY AS PER AMCA/NSF GUIDELINES

What should be the Right Velocity?

Everyone in the industry struggles with the above question and many times, engineers out of their experience or some thought specify velocities at different points, either on top of the door or on the floor, etc...

Air Curtain Manual by AMCA specifies the right velocity parameters. The same is mentioned in NSF Guidelines also.

The velocity specifications as mentioned in AMCA Publication, 222-08 Application manual for Air Curtains, are as follows:

Application Manual for Air Curtains; Section 8.6.1.2

8.6.1.2 ANSI/NSF 37 - Air Curtains for Entranceways in Food and Food Service Establishments. The NSF standard establishes criteria for ACU air performance, construction, design and material type. An ACU construction that complies with this standard is considered by the food service industry to provide effective flying insect protection to an entryway by deterring flying insects from entering through the opening or nesting in the ACU. These criteria can be summarized into basic principles that are intended to create a clean and healthy environment.

AMCA Publication 222-08

Application Manual for Air Curtains

The International Authority on Air System Components

standards specifically written to rate ACUs for sound performance, although many sound standards are applicable and can be used to rate ACUs for sound, such as ANSI/AMCA 300, ANSI/AMCA 301 and ANSI/AMCA 320, to name a few.

8.6.1.1 ANSI/AMCA 220 - Laboratory Methods of Testing Air Curtain Units for Aerodynamic Performance Rating. This AMCA standard defines the test methods that can be used to generate data for the typical types of air curtain's performance. This data can then be used to compare different models for aerodynamic performance. Note that the data generated from the tests described in the standard does not define an ACU's relative effectiveness.

If the data is measured and generated from an AMCA accredited laboratory, the product can be licensed to bear the AMCA Seal (if applied for) under AMCA 211, Certified Ratings Program - Product Rating Manual for Fan Air Performance. The AMCA Seal represents the fact that the ACU has been independently tested by a third party, adding credibility to manufacturer ratings.

The performance data generated, as defined by ANSI/AMCA 220 and simplified here, are:

- Average Outlet Velocity - the mathematical derivation of a velocity flow rate by dividing the air volume flow rate by the air curtain discharge area. This value should be used with outlet velocity uniformity to compare different ACUs.
- Velocity Projection - the average of the peak velocities measured along the ACU discharge nozzle at predetermined widths at specified distances away from the ACU. These values can also be used to determine a Velocity Uniformity at said specified distance.
- Outlet Velocity Uniformity - this is a measure of the consistency of the discharge velocities across the ACU width expressed in a percentage determined by a standard of deviation method.
- Airflow Rate - physically measured by a recognized air volume test chamber using ANSI/AMCA 210, Laboratory Methods of Testing Fans for Certified Aerodynamic Performance Rating.
- Power Rating - this is the electrical power actually consumed by the entire unit (in kW) during the Air Volume Flow Rate; not to be confused with the mechanical energy equivalent to the unit horse power.

T8.6.1.2 ANSI/NSF 37 - Air Curtains for Entranceways in Food and Food Service Establishments. HE NSF standard establishes criteria for ACU air performance, construction, design and material type. An ACU construction that complies with this standard is considered by the food service industry to provide effective flying insect protection to an entryway by deterring flying insects from entering through the opening or nesting in the ACU.

These criteria can be summarized into basic principles that are intended to create a clean and healthy environment. The air performance defined in this standard is geared toward protection from flying insects. The opening types are defined by three categories: Customer Entryway, Service Entryway and Drive Through Window. Each type has its own minimum performance requirement.

The Service Entryway test requires a maximum mounting height declaration and a minimum air velocity of 8.15 m/s (1600 fpm). Velocities are measured within a 75 mm (3 in.) deep by ACU nozzle width wide area broken into 75 mm x 150 mm (3 in. x 6 in.) grids, 0.9 m (3 ft) from the floor.

The Customer Entryway test requires a maximum mounting height declaration and a minimum air velocity of 3.05 m/s (600 fpm). Velocities are measured within a 200 mm (8 in.) deep by ACU nozzle width wide area broken into 50 mm x 150 mm (2 in. x 6 in.) grids, 0.9 m (3 ft) from the floor.

The Drive Thru Window test requires only a minimum air velocity of 3.05 m/s (600 fpm), 1/3 the distance of the vertical opening above the service window counter top. Velocities are measured within a 200 mm (8 in.) deep by ACU nozzle width wide area broken into 50 mm x 150 mm (2 in. x 6 in.) grids.

The design and construction requirements are intended to prevent the nesting of vermin, the accumulation of dirt, debris and moisture; and to provide accessibility for servicing, cleaning and inspection.

The material requirements are intended to ensure that the equipment is resistant to penetration from vermin and wear in the respect for food safety (*i.e.,* the effect of food, heat, refrigerants, cleaning and sanitizing compounds).

Lastly, ACU units can be tested, certified and listed to Standard ANSI/NSF 37 by nationally recognized testing laboratories and certifying bodies that have a food service program. Some of these agencies include NSF and the corresponding NSF Mark, UL.

19

FAQ'S AND ANSWERS RELATED TO AIR CURTAINS

Should the air curtains be mounted inside or outside the doorways?

Generally, air curtains will operate with equal efficiency, regardless of which side of the doorway it is mounted on. However, there are certain exceptions, as follows: Air Curtains should be installed on the warmer side. Inside Installations are done in case of heated Air Curtains when we do not want the cold breeze to come in and want to circulate the inside hot air. Outside installation is required when used over freezer doors because when mounted inside, the fans tend to gather moisture and freeze, eventually forming a snowball around the fan, causing it to lose operational efficiency. Air Curtains installed outside offer a better prevention to mosquitoes and flies.

Do air curtains require a cover when mounted outside?

No, they generally do not require any cover when installed outside, until and unless there is a probability of direct rain or chances of water ingress in the machine. There is standard accessory which can be ordered to make a rain hood or protect the machine.

Is there any difference in sound level when an air curtain is installed inside or outside?

No, there is no difference in sound level of the machines when installed inside or outside, but since air curtains circulate a huge volume of air, in very quiet conditions it may be disturbing. Hence installing them outside gives a better protection and even affects the feel of sound level.

How Far above the doorway header should an air curtain be mounted?

We should install air curtains just above the door header or to a maximum of half to two inches. The closer the top of the door opening is, the more effective the air curtain will be. Extended mounting brackets are available in various lengths so the air curtain can be mounted to clear an obstruction.

In no way Air Curtains should be taken more than two inches above the Door header, generally done in case of fixed glass above the Door. People tend to put it above the fixed glass. In such conditions, air curtain efficiency will be severely affected.

If there is an obstruction over the doorway, how far away from the wall can the air curtain be installed and still function?

Not more than eight inches for refrigeration and fourteen inches for insects. To seal off the ends, twelve to eighteen inch panels made of sheet metal, plastic strips or plywood can be installed on each side of door opening to improve the efficiency of the air curtain. Sometimes the air curtain air outlet nozzle may be installed between the obstruction and the wall. Precaution is necessary to prevent the obstruction from deflecting the flow of air.

What is the average time taken to install an air curtain?

The average time required to install a unit is 90~120 minutes.

Can Air curtains be attached to doors?

Yes, air curtains can be coupled with the doors, with help of a plunger type and magnetic limit switches. The switches can be coupled with any kind of doors, single side, double side opening, Sliding Doors, Automatic Door, high speed shutters, Roller shutters etc.

How long does it take to attach an air curtain with door switch?

The average time required to install a unit is 20-30 minutes.

How do you clear existing lines and tracks over doorway?

There is a variety of optional mounting hardware accessories. Side extension plates are available to further extend the outboard mounting holes. These plates are available in various sizes up to a nine inch extension for both ends of the air curtain. Adjustable mounting brackets and extended wall mount brackets for drum type roll-up doors are also available. These types of brackets are used when the air curtain needs to be mounted some distances away from the wall. The brackets are also available for mounting on the glass and special brackets to connect the two machines together.

When would a vertical mound be feasible?

When installation is not possible over the top of the doorway, the air curtain may be side-mounted on both ends of the door. As per the guidelines of AMCA, in case of side installation the air curtains should be installed on both the sides or in a zigzag pattern to cover the entire length of the door. Yes, the same Air Curtains can be vertically mounted.

Should we take air curtain more than the door-width opening?

We should not take an Air curtain, more than the Door width. Though technically it will not affect, but commercially will not be a right decision. Air curtain length should be more or less equal to the width of the door.

When there is no space above the door, where should the air curtain be mounted?

Air Curtains can be mounted above the Door by cutting a false roof and you should consider following points while doing the same. First, the trap door should be provided for service and secondly there should be a space to suck the air.

Can the door itself be removed and the air curtain allowed to operate continuously 24x7?

Yes, with Air Curtains you can follow an OPEN DOOR POLICY, for your outlet. Air curtains when rightly installed and directional louver set at a right angle, can give a continuous thermal protection and can be installed without a door.

Can air curtains be used to hold in extreme heat on industrial conveyor or Ovens?

Yes air curtains can be used to hold extreme hot air on the industrial conveyor or oven. Actually air curtains are very effective and can prove to be a great money saving tool because a huge amount of money is invested in heating the air through heaters/boilers. When the difference between the ambient temperature and the hot air is higher, losing the air makes an exponential effect on the cost.

The installation of Air Curtains on hot ovens and powder coating conveyors is very different than normal horizontal installation, where the thumb rule says, "We install the air curtain on the warmer side." On the contrary, when the temperature in more than 200°C, the installation cannot be done inside and in such places the installation is done in ambient air with air flowing from bottom to top, with special mounting brackets. Air Curtains are very effective on hot ovens and can hold the hot air inside and various advantages which it can give are:

- Fuel Saving
- Reduced chamber heating time
- Increased conveyor speed results in high production
- Reduced curing time

Can an Air curtain be used over a blast freezer?

Yes, the air curtains should be used on a blast freezer or a cold room door. Generally speaking, if the humidity is high you should prefer to take the chassis in stainless steel and the outer body in Aluminium or stainless steel, with plastic or stainless steel suction grills.

www.ingramcontent.com/pod-product-compliance
Ingram Content Group UK Ltd.
Pitfield, Milton Keynes, MK11 3LW, UK
UKHW021656190726
13853UKWH00001B/287